Jim,
I hope you
guys enjoy.
Love,
Frank

El Gato

Written by: **Frankie Corrigan**
Illustrated by: **Rick Menard**

El Gato was inspired by a REAL cat who lives, poolside,
at a real resort in Cabo San Lucas!

Portions of the proceeds of this book will be given to "No Kill" animal shelters throughout the U.S.

Printed and bound in Canada by Friesens
First edition, 2008
1 3 5 7 9 10 8 6 4 2

www.GetElGato.com

Summary: El Gato (The Cat) lives on a vacation resort in Cabo San Lucas, Mexico. A vacationing bully is picking on his sister and El Gato tries to help but gets in over his head.

ISBN(13): 978-1-4276-2407-9

Dedication

I would like to thank the special woman in my life, Michele, who truly inspires me. I would also like to thank my mom and dad, Mary and Ray. I couldn't ask for more caring and supportive parents.

Acknowledgements

Thank you to Richard Paul Evans for your advice and insight down the long road of the book process. I really appreciate the time given to me. A big thank you to Mike Hasson for utilizing your resources to help with this book. I truly appreciate it. Thank you Rich Coombs for your Graphic Design expertise. I appreciate the love, support and belief in this book from DB, Jessica and to the rest of my friends and family. Thank you to Patty Ramos and to Lauri Loewenberg. Finally, I want to thank the listeners in Utah of our morning radio show (Frankie, DB & The Morning Zoo) on 97.1 ZHT. We've been through a lot over the years and wanted to let you know how much I appreciate your generosity and loyalty.

This is a story about *El Gato*. El Gato lives at a beach resort in Cabo San Lucas, Mexico. People come from all over the *mundo* to vacation in Cabo. El Gato loves people, but some people don't like El Gato and that seems to always get him into trouble.

el (ay-l) **= the**

gato (gah-toe) **= cat**

mundo (moon-doh) **= world**

It was a beautiful *Sábado* afternoon. Every day is *bonito* in Cabo. El Gato was curled up sleeping on one of the many lounge chairs by the pool. El Gato likes *dormir*.

Sábado (SA-ba-thoh) **= saturday**

bonito (boh-nee-toe) **= beautiful**

dormir (dor-meer) **= to sleep**

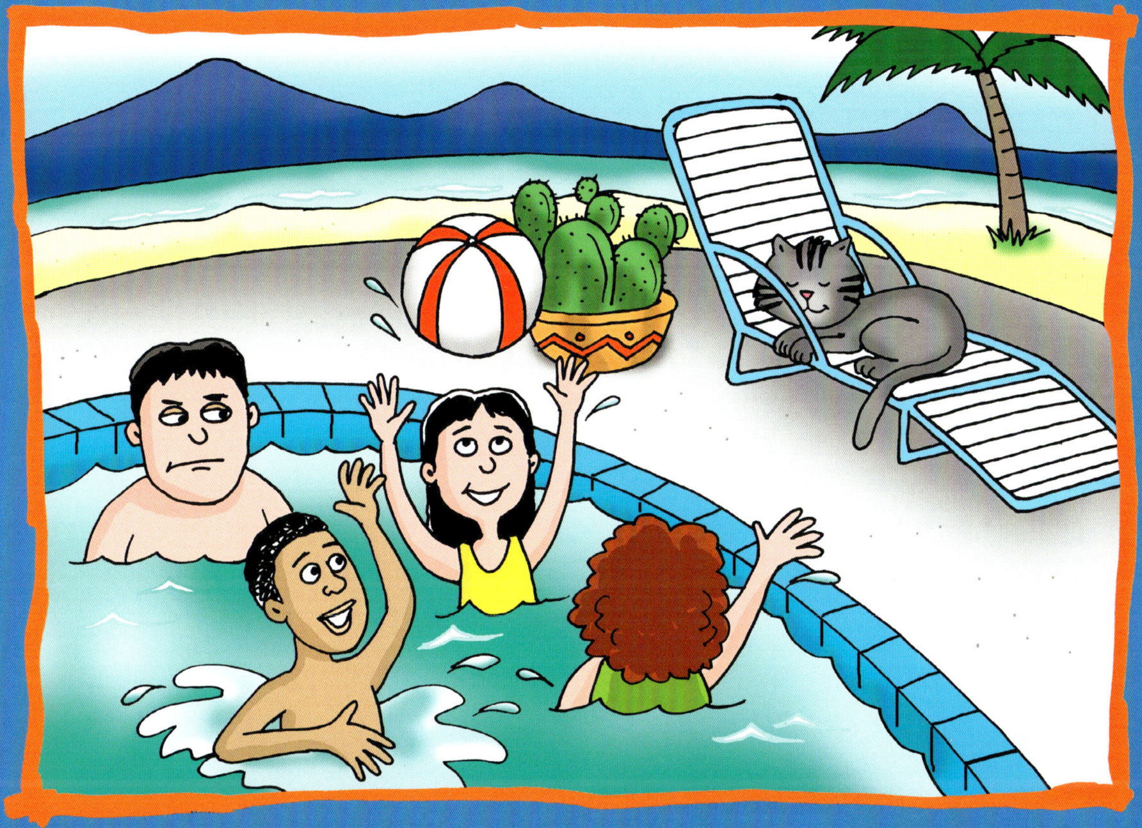

Children were playing and laughing in the *piscina*. One *grito* made El Gato lift his *cabeza* from his nap.

piscina (pea-see-nah) **= pool**

grito (gree-toe) **= scream**

cabeza (cah-bay-zah) **= head**

It was 11 year old Billy Simms splashing his little sister Jenna. The Simms *familia* was vacationing from Cleveland, Ohio. Billy picked on his *hermana* the whole *avión* ride down.

familia (fah-mee-lee-ah) **= family**

hermana (air-mah-nah) **= sister**

avión (ah-vee-OHN) **= airplane**

El Gato was worried for Jenna *porque* Billy wouldn't stop splashing her. Billy was a big BULLY!

Normally cats don't like *agua*. That means El Gato never gets too *cerca* to the pool. Except for this time.

porque (por-kay) **= because**

agua (og-wah) **= water**

cerca (sair-kah) **= close**

El Gato wanted to help but little did he know HE was about to get into trouble. El Gato walked over to the *orilla* of the pool, sat down and meowed to get Billy "The Bully's" *atención*. El Gato thought since everyone likes to pet him, this would solve the *problema*.

orilla (oh-ree-yah) **= edge**

atención (ah-tayn-see-OHN) **= attention**

problema (pro-blay-mah) **= problem**

It worked! Billy saw El Gato sitting near the edge and swam over towards him. El Gato's *trabajo* here was done. He would get a little petting in and be on his way just in *tiempo* to finish his *siesta* by the pool. Or so he thought.

trabajo (trah-bah-ho) **= job**

tiempo (tee-aym-po) **= time**

siesta (see-ay-stah) **= nap**

Before El Gato knew it, he was swimming for his *vida* in the water. Billy "The Bully" threw him into the pool. What did El Gato get himself into?

Billy was laughing at El Gato as he swam in circles. Which side of the pool is closest? Is it this side? Or was it that side? Cats can swim, but only when they have to. He was quickly trying to get out of the pool. *Rápido*. Plus the water was *frio*... *muy FRIO*! Burrrr!

***vida (vee-tha)* = life**

***rápido (RA-pee-tho)* = quick**

***frio (free-oh)* = cold**

***muy (mwee)* = very**

El Gato was starting to worry. The more he kicked and paddled the less he could see *con* all of the water splashing around him. Plus he thought Billy "The Bully" was not through with him. All of a sudden El Gato was grabbed from the *piscina* and he was just about to get the *garros* out. He doesn't like to use his claws unless he really needs to. Get ready to dig them in, he thought. Wait - it wasn't Billy.

con (koh-n) **= with**

piscina (pea-see-nah) **= pool**

garros (gar-rrose) **= claws**

It was Billy's *hermana* Jenna. *Ella* saved El Gato. She waded her way over to the side of the pool and set him down on the ground. Oh the SWEET ground. It never felt so *bueno* on his paws.

hermana* *(air-mah-nah) **= sister**

ella* *(ay-yah) **= she**

bueno* *(bway-no) **= good**

El Gato stood there soaked. He looked like a wet *rata*. That's why cats don't like to get *mojado*, because they look funny. *Gatos* are very particular about their fur.

rata (rah-tah) = rat

mojado (moe-hah-tho) = wet

gatos (gah-toes) = cats

As if El Gato's *día* wasn't bad enough the sound of a whistle shrieked. El Gato, startled, jumped 2 feet into the *aire* on all fours. It was the life guard sitting high in his chair and he saw everything. He pointed to Billy "The *Matón*" and yelled, "You're out of the pool for the rest of the day!" His sister pointed and laughed, "Ha ha, that's what you get for being mean!"

día (DEE-ah) **= day**

aire (air-ay) **= air**

matón (mah-TOH-n) **= bully**

SCREEEECCHHH!
LIFEGUARD

El Gato walked back to his chair, exhausted, as his fur began to dry. The Cabo sun is *muy caliente*.

muy (mwee) **= very**

caliente (cahl-ee-ayn-tay) **= hot**

El Gato curled up trying to finish his nap. He awoke again to more screaming and crying. Here we go again, he thought. Except this time he lifted his head to see Billy "The Bully" crying while his *madre* put aloe on his very *malo* sunburn. Billy was so busy picking on his sister he forgot to put on sunscreen. The Cabo *sol* is very hot.

madre (mah-dray) **= mother**

malo (mah-low) **= bad**

sol (soh-l) **= sun**

It looks like Billy won't be bothering anyone for a while. El Gato put his head back down. El Gato was *cansado*. He had a very eventful day.

The *Fin*

***cansado (kahn-sah-tho)* = tired**

***fin (fee-n)* = end**